Noah's Ark

There are lots of Early Reader
stories you might enjoy.
Look at the back of the book
or, for a complete list, visit
www.orionbooks.co.uk

Noah's Ark

Georgie Adams

Illustrated by Anna Leplar

Orion
Children's Books

Noah's Ark was originally published in 1999
by Orion Children's Books
This edition first published in Great Britain in 2013
by Orion Children's Books
a division of the Orion Publishing Group Ltd
Orion House
5 Upper Saint Martin's Lane
London WC2H 9EA
An Hachette UK Company

1 3 5 7 9 10 8 6 4 2

Text © Georgie Adams 1999, 2013
Illustrations © Anna Leplar 1999

The Orion Publishing Group's policy is to use papers that are natural, renewable
and recyclable products and made from wood grown in sustainable forests. The
logging and manufacturing processes are expected to conform to the environmen-
tal regulations of the country of origin.

A catalogue record for this book is available from the British Library.

ISBN 978 1 4440 0789 3

Printed and bound in China

For Jamie and Dawn, with love
G.A.

In memory of my father
A.C.L.

The story of Noah and his amazing ark is from the Old Testament in the Bible.

Long ago, when the world was quite new, a man called Noah lived with his wife, their three sons and their wives.

Noah and his family worked
hard and tried to live the way
God wanted them to.

But God looked around the world and saw everyone else behaving badly. People were fighting and stealing and being unkind to their animals.

It made God sad.

"Things have gone very wrong in the world," he said to Noah. "I'm going to send the biggest flood **ever**.

I will keep you and your family safe.

When the flood is over, I'll start again with you, and your children."

Noah was just wondering how they would be saved when God told him.

"You must build an ark big enough for you and your family," he said. "Take with you a male and a female of every kind of bird, animal and insect. Make sure you take enough food and water too."

Noah listened carefully as
God told him how to build the
enormous boat.

The ark had to have three
decks, rooms, a window, a door
and a roof, and it had to be
painted with tar to keep the
water out.

Phew! thought Noah.
What a job!

There was no time to lose.
Noah and his family worked
very hard building the ark.

Noah's sons cut down trees,
and made them into planks.
Before long, the boat began to
take shape.

While the ark was being built,
Noah and his wife went looking
for animals.

Mrs Noah made a list: horses,
cows, sheep, goats, pigs, camels,
rabbits, lions, bears, mice,
donkeys, elephants, tigers…

"Don't forget reptiles, birds and insects!" said Noah.

And he made a list too:
crocodiles, snakes, parrots,
pelicans, ostriches, beetles, bees,
ladybirds … ants!

Of course, they found lots
more creatures too.

Remember God had told
Noah to find a male and a
female of **every** kind.

Then they wrote down
everything they would need for
the journey. Things like:

olive oil,

blankets, bowls, wine and
water jars,

barley (for
making bread and
brewing beer),

hay, wheat and oats,

lentils, leeks, onions and garlic,

apples,
melons,
figs
and nuts,
grapes
and dates,

rice,
cheese, fish
and meat ...

They hoped they hadn't
forgotten anything.

At last the ark was finished.
It was enormous.

God spoke to Noah and told
him that the flood would start
in a week. It would rain for forty
days and forty nights.

"Time to load up!" said Noah.

"It will take a week to get this lot on board."

He was right. It took time to get the animals settled inside the ark.

As the last two animals trotted up the ramp, Noah felt the first few raindrops on his head.

Plip, plip, plop!

He took his family into
the ark.

The flood had begun.

The rain poured down. Rivers overflowed. In the cities, the flood gushed along the streets. The water rose over the houses.

Trees were uprooted. Fields became lakes, crops were ruined, and sheep, goats and pigs were swept away.

Inside the ark Noah listened
to the rain falling on the roof.
As the wind blew and the rain
poured, the waves got bigger.

The ark sailed higher and higher
– floating over the trees and hills.
Soon they were drifting over
mountain-tops.

Before long, everything that was outside Noah's ark was drowned.

It rained for forty days and
forty nights, just as God had said.

One morning about six weeks later, Noah looked out of the window.

To his surprise the sun was
shining. It had stopped raining!
But there was water as far as
Noah could see.

God sent a strong wind
to help blow the water away.
The ark drifted about until
… *bump!* It ran into a rock.

Noah looked over the side.

"No damage," he said. "But
I think we're stuck on top of a
mountain!"

They stayed there for many
weeks, with water all around.

Noah sent out a raven, to see if the bird could find dry land. But it didn't.

After a while, Noah tried again. This time he sent a dove. The bird flew a long way and came back to the ark the same evening.

The dove had found nothing. But when Noah sent the dove off for the second time, she came back with an olive leaf in her beak. "Trees are beginning to grow again," said Noah.

A week later Noah sent the
dove out for the third time.

He waited all day but she
didn't come back. So Noah
knew she had found enough
dry land to live on.

Next morning Noah looked
down the mountain.

"Look!" he cried, "The flood
has gone and the land is dry."

The animals couldn't
wait to go outside after
all that time in the stuffy
old ark. Mrs Noah lined
them up two by two, and
led them safely out. Noah
smiled as he watched them
go. They would make new
homes, and begin families
of their own.

51

Then God promised that he would never again send a flood to destroy the world.

"I will give people a sign," said God. "Whenever it rains and there are stormy clouds, I will make a rainbow in the sky. When a rainbow appears, people will know I have kept my promise."

God kept his word. There has never been a flood quite like the one in the story of Noah and his amazing ark.

Did you enjoy reading
the story of *Noahs' Ark*?
Can you remember the things
that happened?

Where does the story of Noah and
his amazing ark come from?

Why did God decide to send
a big flood?

What did God tell Noah to build?

What did God ask Noah to take on
to the ark?

How many days and nights did it
rain for?

What was the first bird Noah sent
out to find dry land?

What was the second bird Noah sent?

What sign did God give as a promise
never to send such a big flood again?

What are you going to read next?

More adventures with **Horrid Henry**,

or go to sea with **Poppy the Pirate Dog**,

or into space with **Cudweed**.

You could have fun on **A Rainbow Shopping Day**,

or explore **Down in the Jungle**,

but watch out for

A Creepy Crawly Story!

Make magic with

The Three Little Witches,

and have
a ball
with

Princesses.

Or follow the star in

The First Christmas.

Enjoy all the Early Readers.